GRAPHIC LIBRARY™

GRAPHIC HISTORY

JOHN BROWN'S RAID ON HARPERS FERRY

by Jason Glaser

illustrated by Al Milgrom,

Bill Anderson, and Charles Barnett III

Consultant:
James M. McPherson
Professor of History
Princeton University
Princeton, New Jersey

Capstone
press

Mankato, Minnesota

Graphic Library is published by Capstone Press,
1710 Roe Crest Drive, North Mankato, Minnesota 56003.
www.capstonepub.com

052013
007383R

 Books published by Capstone Press are manufactured with paper
containing at least 10 percent post-consumer waste.

Library of Congress Cataloging-in-Publication Data
Glaser, Jason.
    John Brown's raid on Harpers Ferry / by Jason Glaser; illustrated by Al Milgrom,
Bill Anderson and Charles Barnett III.
      p. cm.—(Graphic library. Graphic history)
    Summary: "In graphic novel format, tells the story of John Brown's 1859 raid on Harpers
Ferry, Virginia"—Provided by publisher.
    Includes bibliographical references and index.
    ISBN-13: 978-0-7368-4369-0- (hardcover)   ISBN-10: 0-7368-4369-8 (hardcover)
    ISBN-13: 978-0-7368-6206-6 (softcover)   vISBN-10:- 0-7368-6206-4 (softcover)
    1. Harpers Ferry (W. Va.)—History—John Brown's Raid, 1859—Juvenile literature.
2. Brown, John, 1800-1859—Juvenile literature. I. Milgrom, Al, ill. II. Anderson, Bill, 1963– ill.
III. Barnett, Charles, III, ill. IV. Title. V. Series.
E451.G57 2006
973.7'116—dc22   2004029083

Art and Editorial Direction
Jason Knudson and Blake A. Hoena

Designers
Jason Knudson and Jennifer Bergstrom

Colorist
Benjamin Hunzeker

Editor
Christine Peterson

Editor's note: Direct quotations from primary sources are indicated by a yellow background.

Direct quotations appear on the following pages:
Page 6, from *To Purge This Land With Blood, A Biography of John Brown,* by Stephen B. Oates
    (New York: Harper & Row, 1970).
Page 11, from *Life and Times of Frederick Douglass*, by Frederick Douglass (Secaucus, N.J.:
    Citadel Press, 1983).
Pages 13, 15, 18, from *A Voice From Harpers Ferry, 1859,* by Osborne P. Anderson (New York:
    World View Forum, 2000).
Page 24, from original interview text published in the *New York Herald* on October 21, 1859,
    as reprinted in *John Brown, 1800-1859, a Biography Fifty Years After,* by Oswald Garrison
    Villard (Boston, New York: Houghton Mifflin, 1910).
Page 25, from John Brown's original note at the Chicago Historical Society
    (http://www.chicagohs.org/AOTM/Apr98/apr98fact3a.html).

TABLE OF CONTENTS

CHAPTER 1

A NATION DIVIDED

In the early 1800s, slavery divided the United States. Slavery was legal in southern states. John Brown opposed slavery. He grew up in the North, where slavery was against the law.

When he was 12, Brown helped move cattle from Ohio to Michigan. On that trip, he saw a black boy being beaten.

Faster, boy! Keep up!

That boy is my age. Such cruelty is wrong.

Brown never forgot the boy's mistreatment.

As an adult, Brown continued his work against slavery. In 1837, an abolitionist newspaper editor named Elijah Lovejoy was killed by a pro-slavery mob. At Lovejoy's funeral, Brown said that God wanted him to help slaves rebel.

When Brown was 50, the U.S. government passed the Fugitive Slave Act. That law let slave owners capture any black people they claimed were runaway slaves.

Here, before God, in the presence of these witnesses, I consecrate my life to the destruction of slavery.

The law is wrong. That man was never a slave! Government is no friend to the black people.

In 1855, Brown joined his sons who were fighting to keep the U.S. territory of Kansas free from slavery. At that time, territories voted on whether to have slavery or not. A group of raiders called Border Ruffians forced people to make slavery legal in Kansas.

If violence is what it takes to fight slavery, then I will join the fight.

Brown became the leader of a group of soldiers from Osawatomie Creek in Kansas. They chased many pro-slavery raiders out of Kansas.

For Kansas!

For freedom!

For John Brown!

In 1856, some Border Ruffians burned the city of Lawrence, Kansas. The small town was against slavery.

These Ruffians must be punished. I will kill them for this outrage.

That May, Brown and his sons killed five raiders. Brown was then wanted for murder.

They say the men were found with their heads cut off! Did you do this?

I killed no innocent man.

Brown had to leave Kansas. He decided to fight slavery in a new place. Brown grew a long beard to change his appearance. During the next two years, Brown met with abolitionists in the East and North.

I need more weapons to continue my fight.

We shall give you money and 200 Sharps rifles.

I will use them to attack Harpers Ferry.

Harpers Ferry was a military outpost on the border between Maryland and Virginia. Thousands of military weapons were made and stored in the federal arsenal and armory there.

I will take the town's weapons and give them to the slaves. Then they can fight for their own freedom.

CHAPTER 2
BROWN'S PLAN

In July 1859, Brown rented a small farmhouse outside of Harpers Ferry. The farm became Brown's headquarters for the raid. There, he collected weapons and finalized his plans. Brown met with spies he had in town.

Two dozen men can capture Harpers Ferry.

When slaves hear of it, they will join our fight.

Thousands of slaves are sure to rebel. Then the North will have to help them win freedom for good.

For three days in August, Brown secretly met with a former slave named Frederick Douglass. Although Douglass was an abolitionist, he did not agree with Brown's plan.

Join me, old friend. With the town's weapons, we can lead the slaves to freedom.

You are going into a perfect steel trap.

Your plan will turn the country against all abolitionists.

Douglass did not join Brown but other black men did, including Dangerfield Newby. Newby was a free man, but his wife and children were slaves.

These weapons will win my family's freedom.

Word of Brown's raid began to spread through town. At 1:30 in the morning, a mail train reached Harpers Ferry. Brown wanted trains to pass by freely. He did not want word of his raid to reach other towns. The injured guard flagged down the train.

Madmen are taking the arsenal!

Hayward Shepherd was a free black man who worked for the railroad. Shepherd heard the guard say men were attacking. He went to see for himself.

Brown's men thought Shepherd was the guard and shot him. Though badly wounded, Shepherd made it back to the train station.

The guard! He's coming back.

Shepherd! What happened?

Help me. . .

Stop! Hold your fire.

The first person to die at Harpers Ferry was a free black man.

The local militia was forced to retreat. But a few militiamen hid in buildings along the street. The two sides exchanged gunfire.

To the engine house! We must seek cover.

Someone has killed Newby!

As the hours passed, more people rushed to Harpers Ferry. They gathered weapons and joined the local militia. Brown's men were outnumbered and trapped.

Gather any weapon you can find!

This is how we treat murderers.

19

Some of Brown's men begged him to take the weapons and flee into the hills. But Brown refused to leave the engine house. Brown's men began to panic.

We are fish in a barrel in here.

More men are surely coming to join us. When they arrive, these people will lay down their arms.

Realizing he was trapped, Brown sent three men out to stop the gunfire. But the militia attacked them. Only Brown's son Watson returned. He was dying from a gunshot.

What kind of men are they, shooting down my men under a flag of truce?

The deaths made Brown's men nervous. One of them saw a man coming toward the engine house and shot him.

Brown's man had killed the Harpers Ferry mayor.

20

CHAPTER 4
AFTER THE RAID

After his capture, government leaders visited Brown in jail. They questioned him about the raid.

Who helped you? Were abolitionists in the North behind this?

No man sent me here.

Why did you come here?

We came to free the slaves, and only that.

Brown was hanged on December 2, 1859. Only soldiers were allowed to witness the hanging. Townspeople were afraid abolitionists might try to rescue Brown.

This man has divided the country.

I fear we are one step closer to war.

Many people saw John Brown as a hero. On the day of his death, slaves at nearby farms in Virginia set fire to their owner's buildings and poisoned some cattle.

One year after Brown's death, Southern states tried to form a new nation. They wanted to keep slavery legal. By 1861, the issue of slavery helped start the Civil War.

In his final note, Brown predicted that it would take "much bloodshed" to end slavery. At least 620,000 soldiers died during the Civil War. In 1865, the North won the war, and slavery in the South ended. That same year, the U.S. government passed the 13th Amendment to the Constitution, outlawing slavery forever.

More about John Brown's RAID

- John Brown was born May 9, 1800. He was 59 years old when he raided Harpers Ferry.

- Brown had 20 children. One son was killed in Kansas. Two sons died during the Harpers Ferry Raid.

- Secretary of War John B. Floyd received a letter in 1858 warning of Brown's plan to attack Harpers Ferry. Floyd didn't realize that Brown was the same man wanted for the Kansas murders. Floyd ignored the warning.

- Slaves did not join Brown's raid because few of them knew about his plans. Brown did not tell slaves at nearby plantations when he planned to raid Harpers Ferry.

- Many abolitionists supported Brown's plan. One group of rich and powerful supporters were later called the "Secret Six."

- Although Brown's plan was to free the slaves, two free black men were among the first to die in the Harpers Ferry raid.

- Sharps rifles were some of the best weapons available at the time. The capture of Brown and his 200 guns gave Virginia better weapons to use in the Civil War.

- Brown's trial lasted less than one week. The judge did not allow Brown to call any witnesses. The jury took less than one hour to find Brown guilty.

- During the Civil War, Northern soldiers sang a song with the words "John Brown's body lies a'mouldering in the grave. His truth is marching on." The tune for this song was later used for "The Battle Hymn of the Republic."

- A soldier named John Wilkes Booth attended Brown's hanging. In 1865, Booth shot and killed President Abraham Lincoln because he did not want Lincoln to end slavery.

GLOSSARY

armory (AR-mur-ee)—a place where weapons are stored

arsenal (AR-seh-null)—a large collection of weapons

consecrate (KOHN-se-krate)—to promise

militia (muh-LISH-uh)—a group of volunteer citizens who serve as soldiers in emergencies

telegraph (TEL-uh-graf)—a machine that uses electrical signals to send messages over long distances

treason (TREE-zuhn)—to betray one's country

truce (TROOS)—a temporary agreement to stop fighting

INTERNET SITES

FactHound offers a safe, fun way to find Internet sites related to this book. All of the sites on FactHound have been researched by our staff.

Here's how:

1. *Visit www.facthound.com*
2. Type in this special code **0736843698** for age-appropriate sites. Or enter a search word related to this book for a more general search.
3. Click on the **Fetch It** button.

FactHound will fetch the best sites for you!

READ MORE

De Capua, Sarah. *Abolitionists: A Force for Change.* Journey to Freedom. Chanhassen, Minn.: Child's World, 2003.

January, Brendan. *John Brown's Raid on Harpers Ferry.* Cornerstones of Freedom Series. Danbury, Conn.: Children's Press, 2000.

Lantier, Patricia. *Frederick Douglass.* Raintree Biographies. Austin, Texas: Raintree Steck-Vaughn, 2003.

McPherson, James M. *Fields of Fury: The American Civil War.* New York: Atheneum Books for Young Readers, 2002.

BIBLIOGRAPHY

Anderson, Osborne P. *A Voice From Harpers Ferry, 1859.* New York: World View Forum, 2000.

Douglass, Frederick. *Life and Times of Frederick Douglass.* Secaucus, N.J.: Citadel Press, 1983.

Oates, Stephen B. *To Purge This Land With Blood: A Biography of John Brown.* New York: Harper & Row, 1970.

Villard, Oswald Garrison. *John Brown, 1800-1859; a Biography Fifty Years After by Oswald Garrison Villard.* New York: Houghton Mifflin, 1910.

INDEX